UNBREAKABLE

7 PROVEN 3-MINUTE MENTAL TOUGHNESS DRILLS for YOUNG ATHLETES

NEXTLEVEL PUBLICATIONS

UNBREAKABLE: 7 Proven 3-Minute Mental Toughness Drills for Young Athletes

Faith-Fueled Mindset Strategies to Build Confidence, Beat Pressure, & Forge Championship Character

NextLevel Publications

Copyright © 2026 by NextLevel Publications - All rights reserved.

The content contained within this book may not be reproduced, duplicated or transmitted without direct written permission from the author or the publisher.

Under no circumstances will any blame or legal responsibility be held against the publisher, or author, for any damages, reparation, or monetary loss due to the information contained within this book. Either directly or indirectly. You are responsible for your own choices, actions, and results.

Legal Notice:

This book is copyright protected. This book is only for personal use. You cannot amend, distribute, sell, use, quote or paraphrase any part, or the content within this book, without the consent of the author or publisher.

Disclaimer Notice:

Please note the information contained within this document is for educational and entertainment purposes only. All effort has been executed to present accurate, up to date, and reliable, complete information. No warranties of any kind are declared or implied. Readers acknowledge that the author is not engaging in the rendering of legal, financial, medical or professional advice. The content within this book has been derived from various sources. Please consult a licensed professional before attempting any techniques outlined in this book.

By reading this document, the reader agrees that under no circumstances is the author responsible for any losses, direct or indirect, which are incurred as a result of the use of the information contained within this document, including, but not limited to errors, omissions, or inaccuracies, or any direct, indirect, incidental, special, consequential, or punitive damages, even if advised of the possibility of such damages. By using this book, you agree to these terms and release and hold harmless the author and publisher from any and all liability.

Contents

THE MIND WINS FIRST   V

1. THE IDENTITY CODE: 1
Speak It. Believe It. Become It.

2. THE GAME PLAN CODE: 12
Write It. Plan It. Live It.

3. THE BLUEPRINT CODE: 21
Study the Greats. Model the Best. Become Elite.

4. THE VISUALIZATION CODE: 30
See It. Rehearse It. Perform It.

5. THE COMPOSURE CODE: 38
Breathe Deep. Stay Calm. Perform Big.

6. THE QUIET MIND CODE: 47
Clear Your Mind. Find Your Focus. Perform in the Zone.

7. THE LIMITATIONS CODE: 56
Use Less. Train Hard. Gain More.

BUILT FOR WHAT'S NEXT   67

OUR SINCERE GRATITUDE   69

SCRIPTURE SOURCES   70

THE MIND WINS FIRST

What separates a good athlete from a legendary one? It is not just who runs the fastest, jumps the highest, or spends the most hours in the weight room.

At the elite level, everybody is physically gifted. **The true separator, the ultimate secret to greatness, is a mentally tough mindset.**

UNBREAKABLE: *7 Proven 3-Minute Mental Toughness Drills for Young Athletes* is an athlete's blueprint to building an unbreakable mind. It is written specifically for male and female teen athletes ages 10 to 17 who are ready to take their game to the next level.

But let's be completely honest right from the start. **This book is not for everyone.**

If you are looking for a magic shortcut, if you like making excuses, or if you do not want to put in hard work and extra hours, you should put this book down right now. Mental toughness is not handed to you; it is earned. It is built through sweat, discipline, repetition, and grit.

If you are still reading, then you are ready to take on the challenge.

Inside these pages, you will discover the ultimate training manual for your brain. We have broken down the mental game into **7 Proven, 3-Minute Mindset Drills backed by science and faith**.

These are not just motivational quotes. These drills are backed by real, measurable sports science and proven by some of the greatest male and female Christian athletes in the world. Most importantly, every single strategy is anchored in the ultimate truth of Scripture, showing you how your faith, mind, and your sport are designed to work perfectly together.

You will study the exact mental codes used by legends and champions who dominated their sport, including: **Kurt Warner, Serena Williams, Tim Tebow, Carissa Moore, Stephen Curry, Coco Gauff, Simone Biles, Russell Wilson, Clayton Kershaw, Gabby Douglas, Michael Chandler, Sydney McLaughlin-Levrone, George Foreman, Manny Pacquiao, Lionel Messi, and Katie Ledecky.**

How You Will Benefit From This Book: By mastering these seven drills, you will completely transform the way you compete. You will learn how to train your subconscious mind, conquer game-day anxiety, bounce back instantly from embarrassing mistakes, silence the chaotic noise of pressure, control your breathing, and intentionally trigger the "flow state" so you can perform in the zone. You will stop beating yourself up over failures and start playing with absolute freedom, quiet confidence, and unshakeable faith.

The mental armor you build here will not just make you a fierce competitor on the field—it will make you an unstoppable leader in life.

A Note on Your Greatest Supporters: Young athletes cannot reach the top of the mountain alone. Throughout this journey, remember that your parents and family are far more than just your ride to practice or the people who buy your equipment. **They are your greatest supporters, your ultimate safety net, and your biggest fans.** Let them into your mental training. Talk to them about your goals, share your struggles, and let them help you practice these drills.

How to Use This Book: This book is designed to be highly actionable. Read it with a pen in your hand. Buy a notebook to write down the drills and keep it accessible. Each chapter tackles one specific mental code and is broken down into the following sections to give you a complete, step-by-step guide to mental toughness:

Scripture: Every code begins with a foundational Bible verse that anchors the mental skill in God's truth.

Athlete Stories: Real-world proof showing exactly how elite Christian athletes used this specific mindset to dominate their sport and honor God. It includes a summary of how their story applies to you and your sport.

The Proof Behind the Drill: The fascinating, hard science explaining exactly what happens in your brain, subconscious, and body when you use the technique.

The Daily 3-Minute Mindset Drill: The actionable, step-by-step physical and mental exercise you will perform daily to build the skill.

The Mindset Check: Quick reflection questions to help you analyze your current mental habits and apply the chapter to your own sport and life.

Parents Coaching Corner: A special section just for your parents, giving them the exact tools and suggestions they need to support and guide your mental growth from the sidelines.

Chapter Summary: A fast, bulleted recap of the most important takeaways from the chapter.

Closing Prayer: A short, powerful prayer to help you surrender your anxieties and fears and invite God into your athletic journey.

Additional Mindset Tools & Resources: Recommended books and resources if you want to dive even deeper into the science and psychology of the chapter's specific mindset skill.

Your physical training has gotten you this far. Now, it is time to train your mind and develop a mentally tough mindset that will take your performance and confidence to the next level.

Turn the page, and let's get to work.

1

THE IDENTITY CODE:

Speak It. Believe It. Become It.

"Do not conform to the pattern of this world but be transformed by the renewing of your mind. Then you will be able to test and approve what God's will is—His good, pleasing and perfect will."

Romans 12:2

The Identity Code in Action – Kurt Warner

Let's talk about one of the greatest underdog stories in sports history.

Picture this: bright stadium lights, roaring fans, confetti falling from the sky. Kurt Warner stands on the biggest stage in football after winning the Super Bowl. Reporters rush in. Cameras flash. The whole world is watching.

What does he say first? "First things first, I've got to thank my Lord and Savior up above."

That was not a random quote. That was his identity speaking, built many years before.

To really understand the power of that moment, we have to rewind the tape. Before the trophies and the fame, Kurt was just a young quarterback with a massive dream. But his path was incredibly rough. In college at Northern Iowa, he spent a lot of time buried on the depth chart, standing on the sidelines. When the 1994 NFL Draft rolled around, every single team passed on him. NFL scouts looked at him and saw an average player. He eventually got a tiny opportunity with the Green Bay Packers, but he was cut before the season even started.

Think about that. A lifelong dream. One opportunity. Then rejection. Kurt went back home and took a job stocking soup cans in aisle seven of a local grocery store for about five bucks an hour. While other guys his age were signing million-dollar contracts, Kurt was stacking cans and living in a basement. The entire world was telling him his football story was over.

Here is the powerful part.

Kurt did not let those bad circumstances change his identity. He still trained hard every day. He still threw passes. He still prepared like he was an NFL quarterback.

He kept acting like a professional quarterback before he had proof he would ever become one. That is The Identity Code.

Kurt chose to believe he was more than a grocery store worker and an undrafted player. He chose to believe God still had a plan for him on the football field.

Because he made that identity decision, he was ready when the door finally opened. He took a chance playing Arena Football for the Iowa Barnstormers. He worked harder, he dominated, and he stayed ready. Eventually, the St. Louis Rams noticed and signed him as a backup. When the starting quarterback got injured, Kurt's moment had arrived. In his very first season as a starter, he threw for over 4,000 yards, won the league MVP, led his team to a Super Bowl title, and won the Super Bowl MVP.

He went from stocking shelves to holding the greatest trophy in football.

So, I have to ask you. **Who have you decided you are?**

Not who the scoreboard says you are after a tough game. Not who a coach says you are after one mistake. Not who social media says you should be.

Here is the truth every mentally tough athlete learns: confidence does not usually come first. Decision comes first. You choose who you are, then your actions begin to match it. You decide first, and the confidence comes after. It is like stepping into the weight room. You do not wait to feel strong before you train. You train first, and the strength shows up later.

Let's look at Romans 12:2. It says, "Do not conform to the pattern of this world but be transformed by the renewing of your mind." God didn't say, "Wait until the world believes in you, then renew your mind." He said be transformed by renewing your mind. That means change the way you think now. Decide now. Let your mind line up with God's plan before you see proof.

The verse means you do not have to accept labels placed on you by coaches, rankings, critics, or bad moments. When you renew your mind with God's truth, you're making an identity decision.

That is exactly what Kurt Warner did. He did not wait until he was holding a trophy to believe he was called for more.

And here is the best part: you do not have to make that identity decision alone. The same God who opened doors for Kurt Warner will open doors for you in his timing.

So decide who you are. Decide you are disciplined, resilient, and built for pressure. Decide you belong in your sport. Then keep showing up until the world catches up to what God already knew about you.

The Subconscious Mind in Action - Serena Williams

Pressure-packed moments reveal what has been built inside an athlete long before game day.

Think about Serena Williams standing on center court with a championship match on the line. The crowd is loud. The stakes are huge. Millions are watching. Yet she looks steady, powerful, mentally tough, and completely locked in. Her posture says confidence. Her focus says readiness. Her presence says she expects to win.

That kind of mental composure isn't built in one moment. It is the result of years of training the subconscious mind.

Many years before the world knew her name, Serena was a young girl hitting tennis balls on public courts in Compton, California beside her sister Venus. In Compton, the environment was far from glamorous. The courts were cracked and rough. Family resources were limited. Her coach never played tennis. Most people would not have looked there and predicted two global tennis champions.

But inside her home, a different story was being written.

Her father and coach, Richard Williams, believed the mind had to be trained before the body could fully thrive. He constantly spoke greatness over Serena and Venus. He told them they were future champions long before they had ever won a match. He placed motivational reminders around practice areas and in their home. He repeated strong positive words to Serena and Venus until those beliefs became automatic. He guarded what entered their subconscious minds because he knew negative thoughts create doubt and mental blocks if you let them.

That was powerful wisdom.

Your subconscious mind is always listening. It stores repeated thoughts, repeated words, repeated emotions, and repeated beliefs. Then when pressure arrives, it often responds from what has already been stored there.

Serena was intentionally raised to always believe in herself and her abilities, and she only allowed positive, motivational thoughts to enter her mind.

She heard messages of strength, discipline, confidence, possibility, and purpose from her family. She was taught that obstacles were not the end of the story. She learned to see herself as a winner before the results were visible. Over time, greatness stopped feeling impossible and started feeling normal for Serena.

As she grew older, Serena made those habits her own. She spoke confidently about becoming number one before it happened. She visualized winning major titles before she held them. She practiced with fierce intensity so pressure would feel familiar. She practiced positive mental self-coaching before serves and between points. After making mistakes, she refocused on the next point instead of replaying the last one. She learned to replace panic with purpose and doubt with confidence.

That is training your subconscious mind.

The world tries to train your mind every day. It says your mistakes define you. It says compare yourself to everyone else. It says one bad game means you are not enough. It says listen to critics and live in doubt.

But in Romans 12:2 God says to renew your mind. That means replacing destructive mental patterns with truth. It means refusing to let negative thinking camp out in your head. It means choosing positive thoughts that align with confidence, faith, growth, and purpose. It means guarding what enters your mind because what enters often grows wild.

Serena modeled that.

When matches got tense, she did not collapse. She slowed down, trusted her routines, and competed one point at a time. When doubters got loud, she did not shrink. She leaned on years of inner belief and fearless self-talk. When setbacks came, she did not accept defeat as identity. She trained herself to respond, reset, and keep fighting.

Then the world saw the results of her subconscious training. She won 23 Grand Slam singles titles. She inspired generations of athletes. She built one of the most dominant careers in sports history.

Young athlete, you should know that your mind is being shaped right now by what you feed it. Every song. Every word. Every thought. Every phrase you repeat. Every label you accept or reject.

Here is what mentally tough athletes understand: big moments do not invent your mindset. They reveal it. Serena Williams did not become confident when the trophies arrived. She became confident through years of training her inner voice and subconscious mind before the trophies ever came.

So ask yourself: What are you feeding your mind?

The Proof Behind the Drill & Why It Matters

Every athlete is building an identity, whether they realize it or not. The question is whether you are building it on purpose or letting other people build it for you. The greatest athletes in the world do not wait for a perfect game to decide they are champions. They make the decision first. This is what we call the Identity Code.

They choose who they are and what they want to become before the world decides it for them.

The greatest athletes do not wait for success to believe in themselves. They believe first, then they establish mental and physical habits to make it possible. That is how identity works. You do not become confident after everything goes right. You build confidence by deciding who you are, then proving it daily through your thoughts, habits, and work ethic. Champions do not wait for the world to approve them. They know who they are first.

To make that identity stick, you have to understand the most powerful tool you own. It's your subconscious mind.

Think of your subconscious as the ultimate supercomputer that controls 97 percent of your life without you even realizing it. It beats your heart, it breathes your lungs, and it takes over when you are running on autopilot. It controls habits, reactions, body language, emotional patterns, and many split-second decisions during competition.

Here is an important truth: your subconscious mind believes everything you feed it. It doesn't filter the good thoughts from the bad thoughts. It can't tell if your thoughts are positive or negative. It accepts whatever you feed it, so you have to be careful what you consistently tell yourself. Everything you repeatedly say goes straight into your subconscious mind with no filter.

When a young athlete says, "I am a champion," "I am confident," "I am disciplined," or "I stay calm under pressure," it activates the prefrontal cortex, the part of the brain linked to focus, decision-making, and self-control. It also engages the reticular activating system (RAS), which helps filter what you notice and prioritize. That means your brain starts looking for opportunities to act in line with the identity and words you keep feeding it.

Researchers call this self-affirmation theory (Claude Steele, 1988; Cohen & Sherman, 2014), and studies show that athletes who consistently affirm positive thoughts and core values can reduce stress responses, improve resilience, and perform better under pressure. In simple terms, the words you consistently tell yourself, or affirm, can shape how you compete.

Your subconscious mind learns through repetition and habit. Repeated thoughts, routines, and reactions strengthen neural pathways, which are connections in the brain that make behaviors more automatic over time, or on autopilot. This is called neuroplasticity, the brain's ability to rewire itself through repeated practice. That is why visualization, positive self-talk, breathing routines, and calm reset habits are powerful for athletes. When you consistently picture success, speak confidence, affirm positive outcomes, and respond well after mistakes, your brain begins treating those responses as normal.

That is exactly why this drill matters and why we must start right here. You have to take control of the mental programming. Mentally tough athletes do not leave their thoughts to chance. They make an identity decision and then surround their minds with the exact reality they want to create, and they refuse to entertain the negative doubts they do not want to see happen.

3-Minute Mindset Drill #1: Master Your Identity, Build Your Beliefs, Program Your Subconscious Mind

At the start of each day, use this drill to decide who you are, what you want to become as an athlete, and teach your mind to follow that direction. The goal is simple: Make your identity decision before the world decides it for you.

Step 1: Pick one identity trait you want to build right now. Keep it simple and specific.

Examples: Calm, Confident, Disciplined. Focused, Resilient

Step 2: Turn it into one short self-affirmation statement. Write one sentence that starts with "I am." Make it strong, direct, and easy to remember. Write it down and keep it accessible. Examples:

"I am calm under pressure." "I am disciplined in my daily training." "I am confident."

Step 3: Connect your identity statement to a scripture verse from the Bible by writing a short Bible truth under your statement. Use Romans 12:2 as a start. This is your reminder that God can renew the way you think, even when the rest of the world thinks differently. Examples: "With God's truth, I can think differently than everyone else." "My mind is being trained by truth and self-affirmation, not labels."

Step 4: Read both lines out loud stating your identity statement first. Then say your Scripture statement. When you feed your mind with positive, motivating words, you help train your subconscious mind to believe them.

Step 5: Replace one negative thought. Think of one negative thought you have been feeding your mind lately. Then rewrite it into a positive message that you want to become a future reality. Examples:

"I always mess up" becomes "I recover quickly and keep going." "I can't handle pressure in games" becomes "I stay steady and compete with confidence."

Step 6: Intentionally guard your thoughts for the rest of the day. No negative thoughts or words. Only tell yourself what you want your future reality to be.

Step 7: Repeat steps 1-6 every day. Do this first thing in the morning before your busy day starts. The more often you repeat positive thoughts and self-affirmation, the more your mind will believe it.

The Mindset Check

Kurt Warner kept acting like a professional quarterback before he had proof he would ever become one.

Serena Williams was intentionally raised in believing in herself and her abilities and only allowed positive, motivational thoughts to enter her mind. She became a confident champion through years of training her inner voice and subconscious mind long before the trophies ever came.

Reflection Questions:

What kind of athlete do you need to decide to become today so your habits can start matching that decision tomorrow?

What thoughts, words, or voices are you feeding your mind right now, and are they building confidence or creating doubt?

Parents Coaching Corner

Parents, you are the most influential voice in your athlete's life. While coaches focus on developing physical skills, you have the unique power to help train their subconscious mind and support their chosen identity.

Remember that your athlete's brain does not have a filter. It absorbs whatever it hears the most. When you catch them speaking negatively about their performance, gently step in and remind them of their Identity Code. If they say they always mess up, help them flip the script to say they are confident, recover quickly, and keep going. Your steady belief in their chosen identity, especially after a tough game or frustrating practice, is the exact anchor they need to keep their confidence up and their dreams alive.

Make this a team effort. Ask your athlete to share their daily "I am" statements with you and help them write those words on a sticky note or index card for the refrigerator, bathroom mirror or their sports bag.

On the car ride to the game, try not to coach the physical game plan. Instead, ask them to repeat their identity statement and scripture verse out loud to get their mind locked in.

After the game, regardless of what the scoreboard says, praise their effort and reinforce the mentally tough identity they are building.

When you actively partner with them to guard and defend their thoughts and speak positively over their potential, you help them train their subconscious mind and build an unbreakable mindset that will carry them to the next level.

Chapter Summary

Great athletes make an identity decision and then surround their minds with the exact reality they want to create, and they refuse to entertain the negative doubts they do not want to see happen.

Decide Your Identity: The greatest athletes in the world do not wait for a perfect game to decide they are champions. They make the decision first. Choose the kind of athlete you want to become before coaches, critics, mistakes, or the scoreboard decides it for you.

Confidence Follows Action: Real confidence usually comes after you make an identity decision and back it up with faith, daily effort, discipline, and preparation.

Feed Your Mind Wisely: Your subconscious mind has no filter. It believes what you repeatedly tell it, so replace doubt, fear, and negative talk with positive self-talk, affirmations, and words of greatness and confidence.

Train Your Subconscious Mind: Our subconscious mind learns through repetition and habit. Big moments do not create mental toughness; they reveal the mindset and the daily mental habits you have been practicing in private.

Daily Mindset Drill #1: Complete the mindset drill every day first thing in the morning before your busy day starts. The more often you repeat positive thoughts and self-affirmation, the more your mind will believe it.

Renew Your Mind: Romans 12:2 reminds you to reject negative labels, think differently than the world, and become the athlete God created you to be.

Closing Prayer

Dear God, thank You for creating me with purpose, value, and an identity anchored in Christ.

Help me renew my mind each day with truth instead of fear, confidence instead of doubt, and positive words instead of negativity. Train my thoughts to become strong, disciplined, and focused so I can compete with confidence and honor You in all I do. Amen.

Additional Mindset Tools & Resources

Mind Gym: *An Athlete's Guide to Inner Excellence* is a 2001 self-help and sports psychology book by Gary Mack, with David Casstevens. It presents mental training techniques designed to help athletes improve performance by strengthening focus, confidence, and resilience.

2

THE GAME PLAN CODE:

Write It. Plan It. Live It.

"Then the Lord replied: 'Write down the revelation and make it plain on tablets so that a herald may run with it. For the revelation awaits an appointed time; it speaks of the end and will not prove false. Though it linger, wait for it; it will certainly come and will not delay.'"

Habakkuk 2:2-3

The Game Plan Code in Action - Tim Tebow

Some athletes dream. Other athletes write the dream down, build a plan, and chase it with everything they have.

Tim Tebow was one of those athletes.

Before the championships, before the headlines, and before becoming one of the most talked-about college football players in America, Tebow was known for something deeper than talent. He had direction. He had purpose. He had a clear game plan for who he wanted to become.

When he arrived at University of Florida, he was entering one of the most competitive football programs in the nation. Nothing was guaranteed. There were talented players everywhere. Starting jobs had to be earned. Success had to be built.

But Tim did not just hope things would work out. He attacked every day with strict intention.

Tebow became known for writing goals down, reviewing them often, and organizing his days around progress. He focused on becoming stronger, learning the offense, earning trust, and becoming a leader his teammates could follow. Instead of only chasing trophies, he broke his big dreams down into daily process goals.

That meant showing up early. Extra film study. Extra reps after practice. Strength training with intensity. Learning playbooks until details became automatic. Encouraging teammates. Competing hard in every drill.

Those habits and processes were not random. They were a roadmap to his vision and ultimate goal.

He understood that national titles are won through ordinary Tuesdays, hard Wednesdays, and disciplined mornings when nobody is watching. He knew the starting quarterback position was not earned by wishing for it. It was earned through stacking enough winning days together.

That is The Game Plan Code.

Tim's strong Christian faith also shaped how he approached life. He openly trusted God, stood firm in his beliefs, and tried to honor Christ through competition. His famous eye-black Bible references showed that he wanted his platform to mean more than stats.

He understood something many young athletes miss: Talent may open the door, but direction keeps you moving forward.

Tim's roadmap was not glamorous or easy. It was filled with many obstacles. There were injuries. Critics. Huge expectations. Pressure. Tough losses. National spotlight. Constant noise.

But Tim kept returning to the plan: train hard, lead well, stay faithful, keep improving. He did not need motivation every day because the system was already in place.

When obstacles like those start popping up, athletes without a plan panic. Athletes with a well-written plan like Tim's, adjust and keep moving.

Tebow's mindset helped lead Florida to two national championships. Tebow won the Heisman Trophy and became one of college football's most respected leaders.

Let's review Habakkuk 2:2. It says, "Write down the revelation and make it plain." God didn't say to keep the vision floating in your head. He said to write it down clearly. Why? Because written vision creates focus. Written goals create action. Written plans help you stay steady when emotions change.

Tebow did not just want success. He wrote the vision, built the process, and lived with purpose every day.

That is your challenge too. Write the vision. Build the plan. Live it daily. A dream without a written plan is just a wish.

The Game Plan Code in Action - Carissa Moore

Now let's look at a sport where you absolutely cannot control the playing field. Carissa Moore is a five-time world champion surfer and an Olympic gold medalist. In surfing, the ocean is completely unpredictable. The waves change, the wind shifts, and things go wrong in almost every single heat. You can paddle out with a perfect strategy, and the ocean will completely ignore it.

So how does a champion build a game plan in a sport full of chaos? Carissa writes it down. Let me repeat that. She writes it down.

Carissa is famous for her intense journaling habits. She does not just hope to surf well. She actively writes down her vision, her specific goals for the year, her daily action steps, and even her deepest fears. Before she ever paddles out into the water, she writes out her exact game plan for the competition.

More importantly, she writes down her response plan for when things go wrong. If a wave closes out early or she wipes out on a big turn, she does not panic. She simply activates the "If/Then" reset plan she already wrote down that morning. By physically writing her thoughts and strategies on paper, Carissa takes the wild chaos of the ocean and creates a calm, focused blueprint in her mind that she rehearses before every heat. She understands that you cannot control a wild wave, but you can control your own mind.

What does Habakkuk 2:2-3 mean for a young athlete today? God is telling you that a goal kept hidden inside your head is really just a wish.

When God said to "write down the revelation and make it plain," He was giving us a clear path to success. Making it plain means keeping your goals simple and crystal clear. The verse says to write it down "so that a herald may run with it." In your life, that means when you read your clear, written goals every single morning, it gives your mind and body the energy to physically run after them. Even if the success takes some time and not on your intended timeline, you must trust God's timing, don't quit, stay the course, and keep working the plan.

When you write your game plan down, you are telling God that you are ready to put in the disciplined work, while trusting that even if the victory takes some time to arrive, His ultimate plan for your life will not fail.

The Proof Behind the Drill & Why It Matters

There is real science behind why the practice of writing down goals is so effective. When you physically write your goals down on paper, you activate both sides of your brain. The logical left side of your brain handles the step-by-step planning and the daily habits required to reach the goal.

The creative right side of your brain visualizes the outcome and feels the emotion of succeeding. Writing engages both sides of the brain at the exact same time, sending a strong signal to your subconscious mind that this goal is a top priority.

Researchers also study something called the Generation Effect (Norman Slamecka and Peter Graf, 1978). This psychological principle proves that you remember and commit to information much better if you actively generate it yourself, rather than simply reading it. When you take a thought from your mind and physically write it out with your hand, you are forcing your brain to process that goal deeply. You are literally rewiring your neural pathways to start looking for opportunities to make that goal happen.

However, you cannot just write down anything as a goal. You must structure your goals correctly. All goals must be: 1) written down, 2) have a clear vision, and 3) be very specific.

Mentally tough athletes build their game plan using two types of goals: Outcome Goals and Process Goals.

First, you need an Outcome Goal. This is your big, exciting clear vision you want to achieve, like making the varsity team or winning a conference championship. But an outcome goal is not enough because you cannot entirely control it. That is why you must also write down Process Goals.

Process Goals are the daily, controllable actions you will execute to achieve your outcome goal. Examples of process goals are shooting fifty extra free throws each day to improve your shot or watching ten minutes of game film after practice.

Successful athletes also implement an "If/Then" strategy. This is your written plan for how you will react to obstacles or mistakes when they pop up. Things will go wrong, I promise you. What separates great athletes apart for the rest of the team is they don't avoid obstacles, rather they strategically plan for obstacles ahead of time, just like Carrissa Moore.

Here is another quick truth about chasing big goals. You cannot just wait until the end of the season to finally be proud of yourself.

Celebrating small milestones along the way is absolutely critical for building your mental toughness. When you crush a daily process goal, like hitting those extra 20 free throws or finishing those 2 extra shoulder press sets after a brutal workout in the gym, you need to acknowledge it.

Taking a second to celebrate a small win trains your brain to crave more hard work and keeps your energy running high when the season gets tough.

Do not wait for the championship trophy to feel like a winner. Celebrate the daily milestones, because those small victories are the exact steppingstones that build an unbreakable champion.

3-Minute Mindset Drill #2: Write Your Vision, Build the Plan, Stay the Course When Things Go Wrong

At the start of your day, before reaching for your phone or getting in the shower, use this drill to take your dreams out of your head and put them into the real world on paper. A well-written goal and game plan gives you a roadmap to follow, especially when adversity hits. Keep these goals in a notebook or journal to build your foundation of goals in.

Step 1: Write Down Your Outcome Goal. Think of the big vision or goal you want to achieve this season. This is your Outcome Goal. Write it down. Keep it clear, present tense, positive, and specific. Example: "I am the starting varsity quarterback and offensive MVP for the 2026 football season."

Step 2: Write Down Your Process Goals. List two daily actions you can completely control that will help you reach that big outcome goal. Example: "I complete twenty extra minutes of footwork drills after practice to improve my agility." "I add 2 extra reps of shoulder presses in the gym 3 times a week."

Step 3: Write Down Your "If/Then" Plan. Things will go wrong and obstacles will happen. Identify an obstacle that could impact your outcome goal. Create and write down a simple "If/Then" statement to plan your response to this obstacle before it happens. Example: "**If** I miss a shot or make a bad pass, **then** I will take one deep breath, clear my mind, and sprint back on defense."

Step 4: Connect it to Scripture. Write down a well-known Scripture verse from the Bible underneath your goals. Use Habakkuk 2:2 as a start. Re-read and say your outcome goal, process goal, if/then strategy, and Scripture verse out loud. Remind yourself to trust your goal plans and trust God's perfect timing.

Step 5: Make it Visible. Place your notebook and written game plan somewhere you will see it every single day. Keep it on your nightstand, put it in your backpack, or slide it into the cover of your playbook. Read it daily so you can reinforce it in your subconscious mind.

Step 6: Celebrate Your Successes. When you reach a milestone in your Process Goals, acknowledge it and celebrate it with your family. Taking a second to celebrate those small victories are the exact steppingstones that fuel an unbreakable champion.

The Mindset Check

Tim Tebow did not let a devastating loss ruin his identity. He clearly stated his game plan and promised to outwork his failure. Carissa Moore does not let the chaotic ocean dictate her mindset. She writes down her daily plan and her specific responses to adversity long before she ever touches the water.

Reflection Questions:

What is the big outcome goal you have been keeping in your head that you need to finally write down on paper today?

What are two daily process goals you can control right now to start moving toward your outcome goal?

How do you normally react when things go wrong in a game, and what is your new "If/Then" strategy to bounce back faster?

Parents Coaching Corner

Parents, one of the best gifts you can give your athlete is a dedicated notebook or journal specifically for their sport. Encourage them to write their goals down but be careful not to write the goals for them. The Generation Effect only works if they generate the vision and goals themselves.

When you talk about their sports goals, try to shift the focus away from the big outcome goals, and instead heavily praise their process goals. If they want to win a conference championship, that is great but celebrate the fact that they did their twenty minutes of extra footwork today.

When they inevitably have a bad game or things go entirely wrong, remind them to look at their "If/Then" strategy plan. Help them realize that mistakes and obstacles are not the end of the world.

Mistakes are just a signal to activate their pre-written reset plan. By helping them focus on the daily process and the recovery plan, you take the pressure off the scoreboard and put the confidence and power back in their hands.

It's incredibly easy to get caught up in the final score or the end of the season awards. But if you want to help your athlete build an unbreakable mindset, you must become their biggest fan during the small milestones.

When they complete their daily process goals, like doing extra footwork or successfully using their bounce back plan after a tough mistake, make a big deal out of it. Celebrate it! Don't wait for the championship trophy to tell them you're proud. Take them out for dinner or reward them with something special they have been asking for.

Praising those small daily victories trains their brain to value hard work just as much as winning. It shows them that you see their hidden effort, and that positive recognition is the fuel they need to keep executing their game plan when the season gets hard.

Chapter Summary

Write the Vision Plainly: A goal kept in your head is just a wish, but writing it down physically commits your mind to the mission. Remember goals must be clear, present tense, positive, and specific.

Activate Your Whole Brain: Writing your goals on paper activates both the logical and creative sides of your brain to lock in your focus. You are more likely to achieve a goal if it is written down.

Focus on Process As Much as the Outcome: Big dreams are important, but success is actually built by committing to the small, daily, controllable actions. Process Goals are the path to Outcome Goals.

Plan for Adversity: Mentally tough athletes write down specific "If/Then" reset plans so they know exactly how to bounce back when mistakes happen or they run into obstacles.

Mindset Drill #2: At the start of your day, before reaching for your phone or getting in the shower, use this drill to take your dreams out of your head and put them into the real world on paper.

Trust God's Timing: Habakkuk 2:2-3 teaches us to be clear about our goals, put in the daily work, and patiently trust that God's timing is always perfect.

Closing Prayer

Heavenly Father, thank You for the specific talents, passions, and dreams You have placed inside my mind and heart. Help me to take the vision You have given me, write it down, and make it plain. Give me the discipline to focus on my daily process goals and the courage to stick to my game plan when things go wrong. Teach me to trust Your perfect timing, even when success seems to linger. Amen.

Additional Mindset Tools & Resources

Pound the Stone: *7 Lessons to Develop Grit on the Path to Mastery* by Joshua Medcalf. This is a phenomenal book that teaches young athletes how to fall in love with the daily process of hard work, rather than just obsessing over the final outcome.

3

THE BLUEPRINT CODE:

Study the Greats. Model the Best. Become Elite.

"Join together in following my example, brothers and sisters, and just as you have us as a model, keep your eyes on those who live as we do."

Philippians 3:17

The Blueprint Code in Action - Stephen Curry

Let us talk about a player who completely changed the way the game of basketball is played. Today, Stephen Curry is a global icon and known as the greatest shooter to ever live.

But if you rewind the tape back to his high school and early college days, he was not the biggest, he was not the fastest, and he certainly was not the strongest player on the court. He was noticeably undersized at six feet tall and 160 pounds and constantly overlooked by major college programs. Curry played at a tiny school called Davidson College, which was not recruited by NBA scouts.

So how does an undersized guard become the most dangerous offensive weapon in NBA basketball history?

He did not just rely on his natural talent. He relied on the Blueprint Code. Stephen Curry became a master at studying the greats who came before him.

Stephen understood early on that to become elite, he needed to borrow brilliance from the best. He heavily studied in detail two specific legendary players: Steve Nash and Reggie Miller. Curry did not watch them just to be entertained as a fan. He watched them repeatedly like a scientist studying a complex formula.

From Steve Nash, Curry studied the art of balance, pacing, and finishing in the paint. Nash was also an undersized point guard who won two MVP awards by being incredibly quick and crafty. Curry would watch game films after film of Nash and isolate his specific movements. He studied exactly how Nash kept his dribble alive while navigating through giant defenders. He paid close attention to how Nash would shoot floaters and layups off the wrong foot to confuse the defense.

Curry then took those specific mental notes, walked into the gym, and physically modeled those exact off-foot finishes until they became permanently wired into his own subconscious mind and muscle memory.

From Reggie Miller, Curry studied the relentless art of moving without the basketball. Miller was famous for exhausting his defenders by constantly sprinting around screens. Curry engraved Miller's off-ball movement into his brain. He watched how Miller planted his outside foot, set up his defender, and exploded off a screen for a quick shot.

Curry modeled his own conditioning and footwork to mimic Miller's relentless style, combining it with Nash's ball-handling to create a brand new, unstoppable game.

Curry's example is where the power of Philippians 3:17 comes to life. The verse says, "Join together in following my example... keep your eyes on those who live as we do."

The Apostle Paul wrote these words to remind believers that who you choose to look at, and who you choose to model, will dictate the direction of your life. God designed us to learn by watching others. For a Christian athlete like Stephen Curry, this principle applies to both basketball and life. Curry's deep Christian faith gave him the ultimate humility. He knew that his talents were a gift from God, but developing those talents required him to be humble enough to learn from others.

By keeping his eyes on players who had already mastered the skills he wanted, Curry built a blueprint for his own success. He applied Philippians 3:17 by intentionally following the athletic examples of Nash and Miller.

But more importantly, Curry applies this scripture to his spiritual life. He publicly models his faith, points to heaven after every made shot, and writes scripture Philippians 4:13 on his shoes; he is a positive, faithful model for the next generation of young athletes to keep their eyes on.

Stephen Curry did not try to invent greatness from scratch. He diligently studied the best, modeled their skills, and then refined his own game to become elite.

You have the power to do the exact same thing.

The Blueprint Code in Action - Coco Gauff

Imagine stepping onto the legendary grass courts of Wimbledon at just fifteen years old. The whole world is watching you play against one of the greatest tennis icons in history, Venus Williams. Most teenagers would be completely paralyzed by fear, pressure, and self-doubt to play against one of their idols. But Coco Gauff did not freeze. She stepped onto the court with absolute confidence, steady composure, and unbelievable skill. She played fearlessly, and she shocked the world by winning the match.

How does a fifteen-year-old develop that level of elite skill and mental toughness? She used the Blueprint Code. Long before she ever faced Venus Williams on a global stage, Coco had spent her entire childhood studying Venus and her sister, Serena Williams.

Coco did not just casually watch tennis matches on television. She obsessed over the details of her idols. She studied the specific mechanics of Serena Williams's legendary serve. She watched the exact way Serena tossed the ball, bent her knees to gather explosive power, and followed through with her racket. Coco intentionally modeled her own aggressive baseline returns after Serena's powerful style.

From Venus Williams, Coco studied elite court coverage and grace under pressure. She watched how Venus moved with long, efficient strides to track down impossible shots. Coco studied their footwork, their racket preparation and position, and their intense focus between points. She would watch these sequences on a screen over and over until they were ingrained in her mind and then would walk straight onto the practice court to replicate their exact body movements. By studying the Williams sisters, Coco gave her brain a clear visual map for her body to follow.

But Coco modeled more than just their tennis strokes and back swings. She modeled their character and their pioneer spirit. This matches the truth found in Philippians 3:17, which tells us to "keep your eyes on those who live as we do."

For Coco Gauff, her Christian faith is a massive part of her identity and her success. She is incredibly vocal about her relationship with God. Before every single match, Coco and her father kneel together in prayer. They do not pray for a victory. They pray for safety, for the health of both players, and for the opportunity to give glory to God with her talents. Coco understands that true greatness requires a strong model of faith just as much as a model of athleticism.

When the Apostle Paul tells us to keep our eyes on the right models, he is telling us to find people who show excellence, faith, and the character we want to achieve. Coco kept her eyes on women who showed her that a young girl could dominate the world of tennis. She studied their athletic brilliance and anchored her own heart in her faith.

Coco Gauff proves that studying the greats is not about completely losing your own identity. It is about accelerating your growth. She took the power of Serena, the grace of Venus, and combined it with her own unique faith and work ethic to become a Grand Slam champion.

If you want to improve your game, you have to find your elite models, study their every move, and build your own blueprint.

The Proof Behind the Drill & Why It Matters

There is an incredible amount of science behind why studying other athletes rapidly improves your own performance. It all comes down to a special type of brain cell called a mirror neuron, which was discovered in 1992 by a team of Italian researchers led by neurophysiologist Giacomo Rizzolatti at the University of Parma.

Mirror neurons work by firing both when you physically perform a specific action and also when you observe someone else performing that same action, allowing your brain to practice and internalize the skill simply by watching it.

In simpler terms, your brain practices the skill just by watching someone else perform it.

This leads us to one of the most powerful learning tools an athlete can use. It is called the Engraving Technique (Daniel Coyle, The Little Book of Talent, 2012). Engraving is the process of intentionally, repeatedly watching a specific micro-skill of an elite athlete until their exact biomechanics are permanently "engraved" into your subconscious mind.

Most athletes watch sports on television for entertainment. They watch the highlight reels, the big dunks, and the amazing catches. **That is not engraving. Engraving requires deep, isolated focus.**

To use the Engraving Technique correctly and effectively, you must focus on one tiny piece of the puzzle at a time. For example, if you want to improve your jump shot, you do not watch a ten-minute highlight reel of three-pointers. You find a video of an elite shooter like Steph Curry, and you zoom in strictly on their footwork. You slow the video down. You pause it at the exact moment their foot strikes the floor. You rewind it and watch that single two-second clip twenty times in a row. You study the angle of their hips. You study the release point of the ball.

By repeatedly feeding your brain this perfect visual image, you are giving your subconscious supercomputer a flawless blueprint to copy. You are accelerating your neuroplasticity. Instead of walking onto the field and guessing how to move your body, your brain already has a high-definition blueprint map to follow.

Once you have engraved the image in your mind by watching it repeatedly, you close your eyes and visualize yourself doing it. Finally, you immediately go to the gym or the field and physically replicate the movement.

The Engraving Technique builds real skills because it bridges the gap between what your eyes see, what your brain processes, and what your muscles eventually execute.

3-Minute Mindset Drill #3: Study the Best, Model Their Skills, Refine Your Game

Use this drill to actively apply the Engraving Technique. Do this right before your physical practice to give your brain a perfect blueprint for your body to follow.

Step 1: Pick Your Model. Choose one elite professional or college athlete who plays your specific position or has a skill you want to master.

Step 2: Isolate One Micro-Skill. Do not study their whole game today. Pick one tiny detail. It could be their footwork on a specific route, their breathing routine before a free throw, or their hand placement on a golf club. Focus on that one micro-skill.

Step 3: Watch and Engrave. Find a video clip of this specific skill. Slow the video speed down. Watch the specific movement ten to twenty times in a row. Pay attention to the absolute smallest details of their body mechanics.

Step 4: Mental Rehearsal. Close your eyes. See the elite athlete perform the move perfectly in your mind. Now, switch the image and visualize yourself performing that exact same move perfectly.

Step 5: Execute the Blueprint. Walk straight into your physical practice and spend ten to fifteen minutes deliberately trying to replicate the exact skill you just engraved into your mind.

Step 6: Connect to Scripture. Read Philippians 3:17 or another Bible verse out loud. Remind yourself that God designed your brain to learn by keeping your eyes on excellent examples of athleticism and faith.

The Mindset Check

Stephen Curry did not rely only on his talent. He built his game by studying Steve Nash's balance and Reggie Miller's movement. Coco Gauff did not freeze under pressure because she had already spent years engraving the greatness of the Williams sisters into her subconscious mind.

Reflection Questions:

Who are you currently studying and modeling your game after?

What is one specific micro-skill they possess that you can use the Engraving Technique on today?

Are the people you are keeping your eyes on living an example you want to follow in your sport and in your spiritual faith?

Parents Coaching Corner

Parents, you can be a massive asset in helping your athlete build their blueprint. Help them find excellent models to study. Sit down with them and watch game films or YouTube clips of elite athletes but change the way you watch. Do not use the professional athlete's film to criticize your child. Instead, act as a guide. Pause the video and ask them, "Did you see where his feet were planted?" or "Look at how she positions her racket before the serve."

Help facilitate The Engraving Technique by teaching them how to slow down the video clips and focus on the micro-skills. Point out the body language, the recovery after a mistake, and the specific mechanics.

Teach them to rewind and repeat the video until the micro-skill is clear and visual in their mind.

More importantly, remind them of Philippians 3:17. Help them find athletes who model exceptional character, strong faith, and humility, so they have a complete blueprint to follow for both sports and life.

Chapter Summary

Find Your Elite Models: Do not try to invent greatness entirely on your own. Identify the best athletes in your sport and intentionally study in detail how they execute their skills.

Master the Micro-Skills: Greatness is found in the details. Stop watching highlight reels for entertainment and start studying specific footwork, balance, and body mechanics.

Use The Engraving Technique: Repeatedly watch a specific, slow-motion clip of a perfect athletic movement until that high-definition blueprint is locked into your subconscious mind.

Activate Your Mirror Neurons: Your brain practices skills just by watching them. Feeding your mind perfect examples accelerates your physical learning process.

Daily Mindset Drill #3: Complete this daily drill to actively apply the Engraving Technique. Do this right before your physical practice to give your brain a perfect blueprint for your body to follow.

Keep Your Eyes on Righteous Examples: As Philippians 3:17 teaches, deliberately model the character, faith, and work ethic of those who honor God with their talents.

Closing Prayer

Thank You God for the incredible examples of great athletes who have come before me and for the way You designed my mind to learn and grow by watching others. Please give me the discipline to study the details, the focus to engrave the right habits into my mind, and the humility to learn from the best. Help me to keep my eyes on models of strong faith and character, so that as I refine my athletic skills, I am also learning how to honor You with my life. Amen.

Additional Mindset Tools & Resources

The Talent Code: *Greatness Isn't Born. It's Grown. Here's How.* by Daniel Coyle. This is a brilliant book that explains the science of how the brain builds skill through deep practice, modeling, and wrapping neural pathways in a substance called myelin. It works perfectly with the Engraving Technique.

4

THE VISUALIZATION CODE:

See It. Rehearse It. Perform It.

"Therefore I tell you, whatever you ask for in prayer, believe that you have received it, and it will be yours."

Mark 11:24

The Visualization Code in Action - Simone Biles

Imagine standing at the edge of a gymnastics mat. The entire world is watching you. The pressure is so heavy it feels hard to breathe. You are about to sprint down a runway, launch yourself high into the air, flip your body multiple times, and try to land perfectly on a target you cannot even see until the very last second. Gymnastics is a sport where one tiny mistake costs more than a medal. It can even cause a severe injury.

To survive and dominate in that kind of extreme, high-pressure sport, you need an unbreakable mental strategy.

Simone Biles is the most decorated gymnast in history. But her secret weapon is more than her incredible physical strength. Her true superpower is her ability to use the Visualization Code to handle intense performance anxiety and stress and compete with steady confidence.

Long before Simone ever steps up to the vault or the floor exercise, she has already completed her entire routine perfectly in her mind a hundred times. She is not daydreaming of her old medal routine.

Simone uses a highly detailed visualization technique to calm her nerves and prepare her brain for the physical requirements of her sport.

When the pressure of expectations starts to build, anxiety tries to take over. Anxiety makes your heart race, your muscles tense up, and your focus scatter. Simone controls that performance anxiety by closing her eyes and visualizing the exact outcome she wants.

Simone is a mastermind at visualization. She uses all of her senses in her visualization practice. She visualizes the chalk on her hands. She feels the exact texture of the uneven bars. She sees the ceiling of the arena as she flips through the air. She feels her toes gripping the balance beam. She visualizes the exact moment her feet will hit the mat and stick the perfect landing. All done in her mind before the actual routine.

By rehearsing the outcome in her mind over and over, she takes away the fear of the unknown. Her brain begins to believe that it has already successfully completed the routine. When it is time to perform, her body simply follows the mental map she has already drawn in her mind.

This practice of visualization lines up with the truth found in Mark 11:24. The verse says, "Therefore I tell you, whatever you ask for in prayer, believe that you have received it, and it will be yours."

Simone Biles leans heavily on her Catholic faith to keep her grounded. She is known to carry a white rosary in her gym bag, and she prays regularly before she competes. But look at what Mark 11:24 teaches us about faith. Jesus is telling us to believe that we have *already* received the answer before we ever see the physical proof. That is exactly what visualization does for an athlete.

When Simone prays for safety and focus, she pairs that prayer with the mental rehearsal of a perfect routine. She makes the choice to believe in a successful outcome before she ever takes her first step on the mat. She does not wait for the perfect landing to believe she is a champion.

She sees it, she believes it, and then her body performs it. Her faith gives her the courage to ask God for strength, and her visualization is the mental proof that she fully believes she has received it.

The Visualization Code in Action - Russell Wilson

Now let us look at the chaos of a professional football game. There are two minutes left on the clock in the Super Bowl. The crowd is screaming so loudly that you cannot even hear yourself think. Giant, three-hundred-pound defenders are rushing toward you, trying to knock you to the ground. Your team is losing, and the entire season comes down to the next few plays.

Many athletes would let that massive amount of pressure completely crush them. They would start worrying about throwing an interception, letting down their teammates, or losing the game.

But Russell Wilson operates differently. He slows down the chaos in his mind and performs well under pressure by using the Visualization Code.

Russell Wilson works closely with mental conditioning coaches to improve his mental game. He uses a technique called "neutral thinking," but he combines it with vivid mental practice.

Hours before Russell ever gets to the stadium on game day, he has already played the entire game in his head. He sits in a quiet room, closes his eyes, and visualizes the most stressful situations possible. He pictures himself in the two-minute warning, down by four points.

He does not just see a picture playing in his head like on a movie screen. Rather, he makes the visualization real. He imagines the smell of the fresh cut grass. He hears the deafening roar of the away crowd. He feels the rough leather of the football in his hands. He pictures the defense bringing a heavy blitz, and then he visualizes himself calmly stepping up in the pocket and throwing the perfect game-winning touchdown.

Because Russell has visualized this highly stressful moment hundreds of times in private, his brain does not panic when it happens in real life. The pressure feels completely normal to him because he has already been there in his mind.

Russell Wilson's ability to see victory before it happens is deeply tied to his strong Christian faith. Growing up, his father constantly asked him a simple question: "Why not you?" "Why not you to be the starting quarterback?" "Why not you to win the Super Bowl?" Russell took that belief and anchored it in the promise of Mark 11:24.

This scripture tells us that when we pray, we must believe we have already received the blessing.

For Russell, visualization is an act of deep faith. It is his way of telling God that he trusts the preparation and the talents he has been given. When he visualizes throwing the game-winning pass, he is living out his belief that God has equipped him for the biggest moments. He prays for the opportunity, he visualizes the outcome, and then he steps onto the field with total confidence.

He visualizes the victory, he rehearses the full game in his mind, and he performs it in reality.

The Proof Behind the Drill & Why It Matters

Visualization is not magic, and it is not just positive thinking. It is a proven, scientific process called mental rehearsal or motor imagery. There is science behind exactly why seeing a successful outcome in your mind translates to a better performance on the field.

When you close your eyes and imagine yourself shooting a free throw or swinging a baseball bat, your brain does not know the difference between the imaginary action and the real thing.

Scientists have used brain imaging scans to prove that when an athlete visualizes a physical movement, the same regions of the brain light up as when the athlete actually performs the physical movement. Your motor cortex, which controls your muscles, begins firing signals.

A famous study conducted by Dr. Guang Yue at the Cleveland Clinic provided clear proof of this. The study had one group of people physically go to the gym and lift weights to build finger and arm strength. A second group never touched a weight, but they sat in a room and intensely visualized themselves lifting the weights. At the end of the study, the physical group increased their muscle strength by thirty percent.

But incredibly, the visualization group increased their muscle strength by thirteen and a half percent, simply by thinking about it. Their brains had literally strengthened their neural pathways and improved their muscle connections without them ever moving a muscle.

Visualization is a powerful tool for beating performance anxiety.

Anxiety happens when your brain perceives a future threat, like missing a shot or failing in front of a crowd. When you get anxious, your brain pumps stress hormones like cortisol into your body, which makes your muscles tight and your breathing shallow. But when you use the Visualization Code, you shift control away from the fear center of your brain and activate your prefrontal cortex, which handles logic and focus.

By repeatedly rehearsing success in your mind, you make the high-pressure situation feel familiar. You trick your brain into believing it has already survived the stressful event.

To use visualization correctly and effectively, you cannot just casually picture yourself holding a trophy. You must make it very specific, detailed, and use all your senses. You have to see the environment, hear the sounds of the game, feel the equipment in your hands, smell the gym, and feel the excitement of winning.

When you create and rehearse this vivid mental movie, you actually build real physical skills and program your body to get the result you want.

3-Minute Mindset Drill #4: Visualize the Moment, Rehearse the Outcome, Perform with Confidence

Use this drill the night before a big game, or in the locker room right before you compete. The goal is to make the high-pressure moments feel completely familiar before they ever happen.

Step 1: Get Quiet and Center Yourself. Find a quiet spot. Close your eyes. Take three deep, slow breaths to calm your heart rate and tell your brain it is time to focus.

Step 2: Set the Scene with Your Senses. Do not just see the field or court. Make it real. What are you wearing? Feel the uniform on your shoulders. Hear the exact sounds of the crowd or the squeak of your shoes. Smell the air. The more senses you use, the more your brain believes it is real.

Step 3: Introduce the High-Pressure Moment. Picture the exact moment that normally causes you stress or anxiety. Maybe it is stepping up to the free throw line late in the game, or walking up to the plate with two outs. Feel the pressure, but remain completely calm in your mind.

Step 4: Execute the Perfect Outcome. Visualize yourself doing the physical skill with absolute perfection. See your footwork. See the follow through. Watch the ball go exactly where you want it to go. Feel the massive rush of joy and confidence that comes with succeeding.

Step 5: Connect to Scripture. Open your eyes and read Mark 11:24 out loud. Remind yourself that you have actively believed in the outcome before seeing the result. Trust that your mind is now ready to perform.

The Mindset Check

Simone Biles defeats extreme pressure and the fear of physical injury by rehearsing her precise movements in her mind before ever touching the equipment.

Because Russell Wilson visualizes highly stressful moments hundreds of times in private, his brain does not panic when it happens in real life. The pressure feels completely normal to him because he has already been there in his mind.

Reflection Questions:

What specific game time situation causes you the most anxiety or stress?

How can you use your five senses to build a more realistic visualization movie in your mind tonight?

Parents Coaching Corner

Parents, visualization is a free and very powerful tool you can help your athlete develop, but it needs the right environment.

You can help guide them through their mental rehearsals, especially if they are feeling very anxious before a big competition. Have them sit quietly on the couch or in the car. Ask them gentle, sensory questions to help build their mental movie. Ask them, "What does the ball feel like in your hands right now?" or "What positive thoughts are you telling yourself as you step onto the field?"

Be very careful not to add pressure during this process. Do not ask them to visualize not making a mistake. The brain does not filter out negative commands. If you say, "Visualize yourself not dropping the ball," their brain automatically pictures them dropping the ball. Instead, always guide them to visualize positive, successful outcomes.

Have them see the perfect catch. Have them see the perfect shot.

By helping them visualize these positive mental repetitions, you are helping them beat performance anxiety and build a deep reserve of inner confidence.

Chapter Summary

See the Victory First: Mental toughness requires you to see a successful outcome in your mind many times before you ever achieve it in the physical world.

The Brain Does Not Know the Difference: Research shows that vividly visualizing an athletic movement fires the exact same neural pathways as physically performing the action.

Beat Anxiety with Familiarity: Performance anxiety happens when the brain fears the unknown. Visualization cures this by rehearsing the stressful moment until it feels completely normal and familiar in the subconscious mind.

Use All Your Senses: Effective visualization is more than a picture. You need to use all your senses by feeling the equipment, hearing the sounds, and experiencing the emotions of success.

Mindset Drill #4: Complete this drill the night before a big game, or in the locker room right before you compete. The goal is to make the high-pressure moments feel completely familiar before they ever happen.

Believe It to Receive It: As Mark 11:24 teaches, faith requires us to believe we have received the blessing of success before we ever see it. Visualization is a key mental exercise for faithful belief.

Closing Prayer

Heavenly Father, thank You for the great power You have placed inside my mind. When the pressure gets high and anxiety tries to take over my thoughts, help me to slow down and picture the success You have prepared for me. I pray that my visual preparation and my mental rehearsal will allow me to perform freely and bring honor to You. Amen.

Additional Mindset Tools & Resources

It Takes What It Takes: *How to Think Neutrally and Gain Control of Your Life* by Trevor Moawad. Written by the mental conditioning coach who worked closely with Russell Wilson, this book is a great guide on how athletes can use neutral thinking and mental rehearsal to get rid of negativity and perform at the highest level under extreme pressure.

5

THE COMPOSURE CODE:

Breathe Deep. Stay Calm. Perform Big.

"Do not be anxious about anything, but in every situation, by prayer and petition, with thanksgiving, present your requests to God. And the peace of God... will guard your hearts and your minds in Christ Jesus."

Philippians 4:6–7

The Composure Code in Action - Clayton Kershaw

There is arguably no lonelier place in all of sports than the pitcher's mound in a major league baseball stadium.

When you are standing on that elevated patch of dirt, there is nowhere to hide. You cannot pass the ball to a teammate. You cannot call a timeout to ask for help. Fifty thousand fans are screaming at the top of their lungs, the bases are loaded, no outs, and the entire game rests squarely on your shoulders.

The pressure in that moment is enough to make a normal person's heart beat out of their chest.

Clayton Kershaw knows this environment better than almost anyone. As a three-time Cy Young Award winner and a World Series champion, Kershaw is considered one of the greatest pitchers in the history of baseball.

But his greatness does not come from throwing the hardest fastball. His greatness comes from his ability to stay completely calm in high-pressure situations. When the game speeds up and panic tries to set in, Kershaw relies on the Composure Code. He quietly controls his breathing.

If you watch Kershaw closely during a high-pressure inning, you will notice a very specific routine.

After giving up a hit or falling behind in the count, he does not rush the next pitch. He steps off the rubber. He turns his back to the batter. He finds a focal point in the distance, and then he takes a massive, intentional, and deeply controlled breath. You can literally see his shoulders rise and fall. He inhales deeply through his nose, holds it for a split second, and slowly exhales through his mouth.

That deep breath is not an accident. It is a tactical reset button for his nervous system.

When anxiety and pressure hit, your heart rate spikes, vision narrows, muscles tighten, and your fine motor skills are impaired, which ruins the fluid mechanics needed to throw a perfect pitch.

By stepping off the mound and controlling his breath, Kershaw forcefully slows down his heart rate, calms his nervous system, and clears the mental noise. He uses controlled breathing to quiet his racing thoughts before he ever steps back onto the rubber.

For Kershaw, this physical reset is deeply connected to his spiritual foundation. He is very vocal about his Christian faith and how it guides his career.

When he steps off the mound and takes that deep breath, he prays and surrenders the moment and the next pitch to God. He is exhaling the anxiety of the moment and inhaling the peace of God.

This is exactly where Philippians 4:6-7 becomes a real game plan. The verse tells us not to be anxious about anything, but in every situation to present our requests to God. The scripture promises that when we hand our worries over to God, His peace will guard our hearts and our minds.

Pitching in the World Series is terrifying, but Kershaw uses his breathing routine to surrender the outcome to God. He cannot control if the batter hits the ball, but he can control his breath, his effort, and his trust in God's presence. By mastering his breath, he guards his mind against panic and performs with incredible stillness and composure.

The Composure Code in Action - Gabby Douglas

Now imagine a challenge that requires absolute, flawless perfection.

The gymnastics balance beam is exactly four inches wide and four feet off the ground. You have to perform backflips, blind landings, leaps, and spinning turns on a piece of wood that is roughly the width of a standard smartphone. Now add the pressure of the Olympic Games, where millions of people around the globe are watching your every single step, pointed toe, arm position, and to top it off, your facial expression. One tiny wobble can cost you a gold medal. One slip of your foot can end your entire dream.

Gabby Douglas faced this same intense pressure at the 2012 Olympic Games in London. She was trying to become the first African American woman in history to win the individual all-around gold medal.

The stress and anxiety of that historic moment were overwhelming. But Gabby did not let the intense Olympic pressure crush her. She used the Composure Code to lock in her focus and perform flawlessly.

Gymnastics is an incredibly dangerous sport, and fear is a very real obstacle.

When a gymnast gets anxious, their breathing becomes shallow and rapid. This causes their muscles to shake, fine motor skills to falter, and their balance to completely disappear. Gabby knew that to conquer the balance beam, she first had to find her composure.

Before every single routine, you could see Gabby standing at the edge of the mat with her eyes closed. She was doing more than waiting for the judges to signal her. She was actively controlling her breathing and praying.

Gabby used deep, rhythmic breathing to slow her racing heart and quiet the roaring crowd. She would inhale deeply, filling her stomach with air, hold it for a few seconds, and then release a long, slow exhale to force her tight muscles to relax. This controlled breathing gave her the power to stay calm and completely present in the moment, rather than stressing about the final score.

Her mother heavily instilled the importance of faith in Gabby from a very young age. Her family relied on Scripture and prayer to combat fear, anxiety, and doubt. Philippians 4:6-7 was a cornerstone of her mental training. The verse says to bring your requests to God "with thanksgiving." This is an important detail for athletes.

When Gabby stood at the edge of the Olympic mat taking her deep breaths, she was doing more than asking God to help her win. She was using her breath to find gratitude. She was replacing her extreme anxiety with a feeling of thankfulness for simply having the opportunity to compete.

How you can apply this today: When the pressure of your own sport makes your heart race and your mind panic, you can use Gabby's Composure Code to take your power back. By stepping away for just a few seconds to take a deep, rhythmic breath and thank God for the opportunity to play, you physically force your brain to calm down so you can perform at your absolute best.

The Proof Behind the Drill & Why It Matters

When you face a high-pressure situation in sports, your body literally goes into survival mode. Your brain perceives the pressure as a physical threat.

A tiny almond shaped structure in your brain called the amygdala hits the panic button. This triggers your sympathetic nervous system, which is your "fight or flight" response. Instantly, your body pumps adrenaline and cortisol into your bloodstream. Your heart rate skyrockets, your muscles get stiff, fine motor skills falter, and your breathing becomes very fast and shallow. In sports, this is what causes athletes to panic and their performance drops.

But there is a scientific hack to override this panic, and it is built right into your own body. It is your breath.

Controlled breathing is the only automatic function of your body that you can consciously control. When you take a deep, slow breath, you activate your parasympathetic nervous system. This is your "rest and digest" mode. Deep breathing also stimulates the vagus nerve, which runs from your brain all the way down to your abdomen. When the vagus nerve is activated by a slow exhale, it sends a chemical signal directly to your heart to slow down. It literally tells your brain that you are safe and to calm down.

Sports psychologists and elite military units, like the US Navy SEALs, use a specific technique called Box Breathing to combat extreme stress in the field.

Box breathing is a simple but incredibly powerful technique that involves four equal steps:

Step 1 - inhaling deeply through your nose for four seconds

Step 2 - holding that breath for four seconds

Step 3 - slowly exhaling through your mouth for four seconds

Step 4 - and then holding your lungs empty for a final four seconds

While the rhythm is rooted in ancient breathing practices, the modern "Box Breathing" method used by athletes today was popularized by former U.S. Navy SEAL Commander Mark Divine. He taught this tactical breathing method to help elite soldiers control their heart rates, master their fear, and maintain laser-focus in the middle of extreme, high-stress combat situations—and it works the exact same way for you in the middle of a high-pressure game.

Box breathing regulates the oxygen and carbon dioxide levels in your blood, which instantly lowers your blood pressure and brings your prefrontal cortex back online. Your prefrontal cortex is the logical, decision-making part of your brain.

If you need an instant reset button in the middle of a fast-paced game, like basketball or soccer, try a technique popularized by Stanford neurobiologist Dr. Andrew Huberman called "the physiological sigh". This is a hardwired breathing pattern scientifically proven to be the fastest way to calm your nervous system in real time.

To do it, take a deep breath in through your nose, followed immediately by a second, shorter inhale to fully expand your lungs, and then release a long, slow exhale through your mouth. That double inhale pops open tiny air sacs in your lungs, allowing you to quickly offload stress inducing carbon dioxide. This instantly lowers your heart rate and brings your logical, focused brain right back online when the pressure gets too high. It's the best technique for a quick reset.

By using these controlled breathing techniques, you can physically force your brain to stop panicking. You can lower the stress hormones in your body, reduce your heartrate, and return your muscles and skills to a state of relaxed readiness.

This is exactly why mastering your breath significantly improves your performance. A calm body creates a clear mind, and a clear mind executes at an elite level.

3-Minute Mindset Drill #5: Control Your Breathing, Calm the Moment, Excel Under Pressure

This is the Box Breathing technique. Use this drill right before the game starts, during a timeout, or between innings to hit the reset button on your nervous system.

Step 1: Find Your Posture. Stand up straight or sit tall with your shoulders back. You have to open up your chest so your lungs can fully expand.

Step 2: The Inhale (4 Seconds). Close your mouth and breathe in deeply through your nose for a slow count of four. Feel your stomach expand outward like a balloon. Do not just lift your shoulders.

Step 3: The Hold (4 Seconds). Hold your breath at the very top for a slow count of four. Stay completely relaxed while holding the air in your lungs.

Step 4: The Exhale (4 Seconds). Open your mouth and slowly blow the air out for a count of four. Imagine you are blowing out a candle through a straw. Feel your muscles instantly relax.

Step 5: The Empty Hold (4 Seconds). Keep your lungs completely empty and hold your breath out for a final count of four.

Step 6: Connect to Scripture. As you complete the box, repeat the promise of Philippians 4:7 in your mind. Tell yourself, "God's peace is guarding my mind."

Step 7: Repeat the Box. Complete this entire four step cycle at least four times in a row. It takes exactly one minute to completely reset your nervous system and regain your composure.

Step 8: The Instant In-Game Reset. You won't always have a full minute to practice box breathing during a fast-paced game. When you need a quick reset in the middle of the action, use the physiological sigh. Take a deep breath in through your nose, followed immediately by a second, quick inhale to completely fill your lungs. Then, release a long, slow exhale through your mouth. You're ready for the next play.

The Mindset Check

Clayton Kershaw dominates the pitcher's mound because he uses a deep, intentional breath to reset his nervous system between pitches. Gabby Douglas handled the pressure of the Olympics by using rhythmic breathing and a thankful heart to calm her nerves before stepping onto the beam.

Reflection Questions:

Think about your last big mistake in a game. How did your breathing change, and how did your body feel in that moment of panic?

When is the best specific time during your competition to step away and use the Box Breathing drill?

Parents Coaching Corner

Parents, one of the most common things we yell from the sidelines when our kids are struggling is, "Just calm down!"

But here is a psychological truth you need to know. Telling a panicked athlete to calm down almost never works because their body is physically stuck in a fight or flight response. They literally cannot calm down until their nervous system resets.

Instead of telling them to calm down, you need to help them co-regulate.

If they look to you from the sidelines in a panic, do not focus on the mistake they just made. Look them in the eyes and say, "Breathe. Control your breathing."

Remind them to perform the Box Breathing technique, if they are between innings or in a timeout, or the physiological sigh if they are in game mode.

By reminding them to control their physical breathing, you help them lower their heart rate and get their brain back on track. Your calm presence and guided breathing will be their anchor in a stressful game.

Chapter Summary

Your Breath is Your Remote Control: Controlled breathing is the fastest and most effective way to consciously take control of your racing heart and panicked mind.

Beat the Fight or Flight Response: Extreme pressure triggers stress hormones and tight muscles. Deep breathing activates the parasympathetic nervous system, telling your body it is safe to relax and perform.

Master the Box Breathing Technique: Inhale for four seconds, hold for four seconds, exhale for four seconds, and hold empty for four seconds. This pattern brings absolute calm to a chaotic moment.

The Instant In-Game Reset: When you need an immediate reset during a fast-paced game, use the physiological sigh—a double inhale followed by a long, slow exhale—to instantly lower your heart rate and bring your focused brain back online.

Mindset Drill #5: Complete the Box Breathing drill right before the game starts, during a timeout, or between innings to hit the reset button on your nervous system. Use the physiological sigh technique during fast-paced moments in a game.

Exhale the Anxiety, Inhale the Peace: Use your breathing routine as a physical form of prayer. Breathe in, exhale, and let go of the worries you cannot control and trust God that he is guarding your mind and the preparing you for the next play.

Closing Prayer

Dear Lord, thank You for the breath in my lungs and the ability to play the sport I love. When the pressure of the game feels too heavy and my mind starts to panic, remind me to pause and control my breathing. Help me to stop worrying about the outcome and instead present my requests to You with a thankful heart. I ask that Your perfect peace would guard my mind and calm my racing heart, so that I can perform with absolute composure. Amen.

Additional Mindset Tools & Resources

Breath: *The New Science of a Lost Art* by James Nestor. This is an incredible, science-backed book that explains exactly how humans have lost the ability to breathe correctly, and how returning to proper, deep nasal breathing can radically transform your health, athletic endurance, and mental composure.

6

THE QUIET MIND CODE:

Clear Your Mind. Find Your Focus. Perform in the Zone.

"You will keep in perfect peace those whose minds are steadfast, because they trust in You."

Isaiah 26:3

The Quiet Mind Code in Action - Michael Chandler

There is no sport on earth that is quite as chaotic, loud, and physically dangerous as mixed martial arts (MMA). When a fighter steps inside the steel cage of the UFC Octagon, they are locked in with another highly trained athlete whose sole objective is to knock them unconscious. The crowd is deafening, the bright lights are blinding, and the physical pressure is unimaginably high.

In an environment built on absolute violence and chaos, you would think a fighter needs to be angry, loud, and raging to survive.

Michael Chandler, the complete opposite.

Michael Chandler is a three-time Bellator Lightweight Champion and top UFC contender who operates completely differently. He does not rely on anger. **He relies on a quiet mind and prayer.**

Chandler is known for his explosive power and his relentless wrestling pace, but his greatest weapon is his daily meditation practice.

To survive the extreme stress of a cage fight, Chandler deliberately trains his mind to find absolute stillness. Hours before the referee ever starts the fight, Chandler wakes up in the pitch dark of the early morning. Before he looks at his phone, before he talks to his coaches, and before he starts his grueling physical training, he sits in complete silence. He spends significant time meditating, controlling his breath, praying, and silencing the noise of the outside world.

When you are a professional fighter, anxiety and fear are very real.

You worry about getting knocked out, losing your ranking, or disappointing your family. Chandler uses meditation to intentionally clear out those negative, stressful thoughts. He sits quietly, closes his eyes, and focuses strictly on the rhythm of his breathing. When a thought about losing pops into his head, he does not panic. He simply acknowledges it and lets it pass, and he brings his focus right back to his breath.

By practicing this quiet stillness every single day, he trains his brain to stay calm in the middle of chaos. When he finally steps into the Octagon, his mind is not racing. His mind is quiet, which allows his body to completely take over and perform in a highly focused "flow state." He does not overthink his punches. He just flows.

This quiet, unstoppable focus is deeply rooted in his Christian faith. Chandler is incredibly outspoken about his relationship with God, and he openly credits his faith for his mental toughness. This brings us right to the truth of Isaiah 26:3. The verse promises that God will keep us in perfect peace when our minds are steadfast, because we trust in Him.

To have a steadfast mind means to have a mind that is firmly fixed and not easily distracted by fear, stress, anxiety, or chaos. For Chandler, meditation is more than an empty mental exercise. It is a time to fix his steadfast mind on God.

When he sits in silence and prayer, he is actively trusting that God has equipped him for the battle ahead. He is laying down the anxiety of the fight and trading it for the perfect peace of Christ.

Chandler's quiet mind gives him the composure to walk into a steel cage with a smile on his face, and he fully trusts his preparation and his Creator.

Young athlete, uou might never step inside a mixed martial arts cage, but the pressure you face as a young athlete is very real. Between the expectations of your coaches, the noise of social media, and the pressure you put on yourself, your mind can easily become a chaotic, noisy place.

When your mind is loud and cluttered with worries about the scoreboard or what other people think, your body becomes tight and slow.

Michael Chandler proves that true toughness is not about being the loudest or the angriest person in the room. True mental toughness is the ability to find quiet stillness when everything around you is going crazy.

If a professional cage fighter needs daily silence to perform at his best, you need it too. Taking just a few minutes a day to silence your phone, close your eyes, and quiet your thoughts will radically change how you handle the pressure of your own sport.

The Quiet Mind Code in Action - Sydney McLaughlin-Levrone

The 400-meter hurdles is often called the most painful race in track and field. You have to sprint at absolute top speed for a full lap around the track, while flawlessly jumping over ten massive hurdles when your legs are burning and your lungs are screaming for oxygen. One slight miscalculation in your steps, one slight hesitation in your mind, and you will crash into a hurdle and lose the race.

Sydney McLaughlin-Levrone is the undisputed queen of this race.

She is an Olympic gold medalist and has broken her own world record multiple times. When you watch her run, she does not look like she is struggling. She looks like she is gliding. She looks like she is running in a completely different dimension than everyone else.

That effortless performance is called running in "the zone" or the "flow state." But Sydney did not always run with that kind of freedom.

Earlier in her career, Sydney struggled with the pressure of being a young prodigy. The expectations of the entire country were on her shoulders. Before big races, her mind would race with anxiety. She felt the heavy burden of having to be perfect. When your mind is cluttered with the stress of perfection, it blocks your body from getting into that flow state. The flow state requires absolute focus and trust, and anxiety is the opposite of focus and trust. Sydney realized she had to shift her mindset and clear the mental noise to reach her full potential.

She changed her routine by using meditation, journaling, and prayer to handle the pressure of the track world.

Before she steps into the starting blocks, you will often see her with her eyes closed, seemingly in her own world. She is not hyping herself up with aggressive thoughts. She is quietly meditating on Scripture and calming her mind.

She blocks out the roaring stadium and focuses entirely on the present moment. She stops worrying about the finish line and simply focuses on her breath, God, and the very first hurdle.

Sydney's transformation into an unbreakable world record holder came through her spiritual surrender. She took the promise of Isaiah 26:3 and made it her ultimate game plan. The verse says God gives perfect peace to those who trust in Him.

Sydney publicly admits that when she used to trust in her own ability to be perfect, she was filled with anxiety. But when she shifted her focus, quieted her mind, and placed her trust entirely in God, the anxiety disappeared.

She began running simply to glorify God, rather than running to please the fans or the critics.

Her meditation and prayer became the tool she used to make her mind steadfast. By clearing out the fear of failure and replacing it with the perfect peace of God, her body was finally free to do exactly what it was trained to do.

When the starting gun goes off, Sydney does not have to overthink her stride. Her mind is completely quiet, so her physical training can take over perfectly.

Track and field is a sport where you spend a lot of time trapped inside your own head. But no matter what sport you play, **overthinking is the ultimate enemy of great performance.**

When you step up to the plate, the free throw line, or the starting blocks and start overthinking your mechanics, you interrupt the natural flow of your body.

Sydney's story teaches us that perfection is a terrible goal because it creates anxiety. Your goal should be to find a quiet mind before your performance. You must learn how to let go of the pressure of expectations and simply trust the hard work you have already put in.

When you quiet your mind and trust your training, you allow your body to perform instinctively. A quiet mind is the key to unlocking "the zone."

The Proof Behind the Drill & Why It Matters

Meditation and clearing your mind is more than a spiritual practice. It is a highly researched, scientifically proven method for improving athletic performance. When an athlete gets "in the zone" or enters the "flow state," a very specific biological shift happens in the brain.

The concept of the flow state was famously researched by psychologist Dr. Mihaly Csikszentmihalyi. He discovered that when athletes perform at their absolute peak, they experience something called "transient hypofrontality." The prefrontal cortex, which is the part of your brain responsible for overthinking, analyzing, and self-doubt, actually powers down and gets quiet. At the same time, your brain waves shift from fast, anxious Beta waves into smooth, calm Alpha and Theta waves. When the overthinking part of your brain gets quiet, your subconscious mind and muscle memory are allowed to completely take over. Your reaction time gets faster, your movements become fluid, and you perform effortlessly.

Meditation is the specific training tool you use to achieve this quiet mind state on command.

A famous study conducted by neuroscientist Sara Lazar at Harvard University showed the incredible physical effects of meditation on the brain. The study proved that regular meditation actually shrinks the amygdala, which is the fear and anxiety center of the brain. At the same time, it thickens the areas of the brain associated with focus and emotional control.

When you meditate, you are practicing the art of focusing on one single thing, like your breath, and ignoring distractions. You sit quietly, eyes closed, and when a stressful thought about an upcoming game enters your mind, you do not engage with it. You simply let it pass by like a cloud in the sky and return your focus to your breathing. By doing this repeatedly, you are literally rewiring your brain to ignore stressful noise.

This helps with performance anxiety because it teaches your brain that a stressful thought is just a thought, not a physical threat. When you master meditation, you can step into a high-pressure game, quickly quiet your mind, shut down the fear center, and trigger the flow state exactly when you need it most.

3-Minute Mindset Drill #6: Silence the Noise, Get In the Flow, Trust Your Training

Use this drill daily in a quiet room at home, and eventually, you can use a shortened version on the bench or sidelines right before you compete to lock into the flow zone.

Step 1: Find Your Quiet Space. Sit down comfortably in a quiet room. Set a timer for 3 minutes. Put your phone away. Rest your hands on your lap, sit up tall, and gently close your eyes.

Step 2: Set The Anchor. Your anchor is the one thing you will focus your mind on. It can be the physical feeling of air going in and out of your nose, or it can be a visual of a peaceful ocean or a calm river.

Step 3: Breathe and Focus. Take slow, natural breaths. In through your nose, out through your mouth. Focus one hundred percent of your attention on your anchor. Feel the breath enter your body and feel it leave your body.

Step 4: The Cloud Technique. Within seconds, a random thought or worry will pop into your head. That is totally normal. Do not get mad at yourself. Imagine that thought is just a cloud passing across the sky. Acknowledge it, let it drift away, and immediately bring your focus back to your anchor.

Step 6: The Flow Trigger. When the timer goes off, before you open your eyes, create a physical trigger to lock in this calm state. Squeeze your right fist tightly for three seconds, then release it. Over time, your brain will associate squeezing your fist with a quiet, focused mind, allowing you to trigger the flow state on the field instantly.

The Mindset Check

Michael Chandler silences the chaos of the MMA cage by starting his day with quiet meditation, trusting God to give him peace in the storm. Sydney McLaughlin-Levrone broke world records by refusing to overthink her race, choosing instead to quiet her mind, trust her training, and run completely free for God's glory.

Reflection Questions:

What are the loudest, most distracting thoughts that usually pop into your head right before a competition?

How would your performance change if you could instantly let go of your mistakes like a passing cloud instead of obsessing over them?

Are you truly trusting your physical training, or are you letting anxiety block you from reaching the flow state?

Parents Coaching Corner

Parents, the modern young athlete is bombarded by constant noise.

Between smartphones, social media, video games, and intense sports schedules, their brains rarely get a moment of true silence and calm.

If you want to help them find their flow state, you must help them create a quiet environment.

Before a big game, our instinct is often to pump our kids up. We play loud, aggressive music in the car or give them intense motivational speeches about how important the game is.

But for many athletes, this extra noise just creates more anxiety.

Instead, try creating a "quiet zone" on the ride to the game. Turn the radio off. Encourage them to close their eyes and practice their breathing and meditation drills.

Tell them to trust the work they have already put in. When you help them silence the external noise, you give their brain the space it needs to find total focus and step onto the field with a peaceful, unbreakable mindset.

Chapter Summary

Silence is a Weapon: A quiet mind is not a weakness. It is the best way to slow down chaotic, high-pressure situations and find your focus.

Overthinking Kills Performance: When you obsess over mistakes or try to be perfect, you block your mind and body from performing the skills you have already practiced.

The Flow State Requires Trust: To get into the zone, the thinking part of your brain must power down so your subconscious mind and muscle memory can take over. You have to fully trust your training.

Meditation Rewires the Brain: Scientifically, daily meditation shrinks the fear center of the brain and trains you to let go of stressful distractions instantly.

Daily Mindset Drill #6: Complete this drill daily in a quiet room at home, with no phone, just a timer. You can also use a shortened version on the bench or sidelines right before you compete to lock into the flow zone.

Steadfast Minds Find Perfect Peace: Based on Isaiah 26:3, when you intentionally quiet your mind and fix your focus on God, He replaces your performance anxiety with perfect, unshakeable peace.

Closing Prayer

Dear God, thank You for the amazing way You designed my mind and body to work together. When the noise of the game gets too loud and the pressure of expectations makes my mind race, help me to find quiet stillness in You. Teach me how to stop overthinking and start trusting the preparation You have helped me build. Let me play freely, with a quiet mind, and give all the glory to You. Amen.

Additional Mindset Tools & Resources

The Mindful Athlete: *Secrets to Pure Performance* by George Mumford. Written by the sports psychology legend who taught mindfulness and meditation to icons like Michael Jordan and Kobe Bryant, this book is the best resource on how athletes can use meditation to embrace the present moment, quiet the mind, and reach pure performance in the zone.

7

THE LIMITATIONS CODE:

Use Less. Train Hard. Gain More.

"We are hard pressed on every side, but not crushed; perplexed, but not in despair; persecuted, but not abandoned; struck down, but not destroyed."

2 Corinthians 4:8-9

Limitation 1: Training With Less - George Foreman

When most young athletes think about getting better, they immediately think about getting more. They want the newest cleats, the most expensive bat, a high-tech private trainer, private lessons, and a massive indoor gym. But more is not always better.

One of the most powerful heavyweight boxing champions in history proved that true greatness is often built by training with less.

George Foreman won an Olympic gold medal and became the heavyweight champion of the world in his early twenties.

But his most extraordinary physical achievement happened twenty years later. At age forty-five, Foreman decided to make a comeback to professional boxing.

He had loads of money, but he did not go to a multi-million-dollar performance facility to prepare. He went back to the absolute basics. Foreman trained by chopping down massive trees with a heavy axe. He dug deep holes in the dirt with a shovel. He harnessed himself to a Jeep and pulled it up a hill using only his raw leg strength.

He intentionally stripped away all the modern luxuries and trained with the bare minimum to build unstoppable, raw power.

Foreman's physical comeback was also fueled by a major spiritual transformation. During his ten-year break from boxing, Foreman became a born-again Christian and an ordained minister.

When we look at 2 Corinthians 4:8-9, we see a picture of someone who is hard pressed and struck down but not destroyed.

Foreman lived this out.

He faced the huge limitations of his older age and his lack of fancy equipment, but his faith in God kept him from being crushed by those obstacles. He trusted that God would multiply his raw, gritty effort.

As a young athlete, you do not need a three-hundred-dollar piece of equipment to outwork your competition. If you do not have access to a perfect field, run hills in the grass. If you do not have a fancy batting cage, hit off a basic tee in your garage until your hands blister.

Training with less strips away your excuses and forces you to build raw, gritty mental toughness that cannot be bought in a sporting goods store or learned from a private trainer.

Limitation 2: Training Tough - Manny Pacquiao

If you want to become unbreakable under the bright lights, you have to learn how to survive in rough conditions.

Manny Pacquiao is the only boxer in history to win world titles in eight different weight divisions. He is a boxing icon with lightning-fast hands and a legendary tough chin. But Pacquiao did not develop that elite toughness in a pristine, climate-controlled environment. He developed it by intentionally training rough.

Growing up in extreme poverty in the Philippines, Pacquiao had absolutely nothing. When I say nothing, I mean nothing. He slept on cardboard on the streets and started boxing as a young teenager just to earn enough money to buy rice for his entire family.

He did not have a regulation boxing ring. He trained in the dirt. He did not have custom fitted boxing shoes. He trained in raggedy shorts and sparred barefoot.

He hit heavy bags that were completely rock hard because they were filled with cheap sand or rags. He fought in dusty, hot, uneven environments.

By practicing in very rough conditions, Pacquiao forced his body and his mind to adapt to extreme discomfort. When he finally made it to the professional level, fighting in a perfect, padded, air-conditioned ring felt incredibly easy because he was so used to surviving the absolute worst conditions.

Pacquiao's ability to absorb punishment and keep moving forward comes from his strong Christian faith. He is a devout believer who reads his Bible daily and openly preaches the Gospel. The promise of 2 Corinthians 4:8-9 perfectly describes his journey.

He was persecuted by poverty and struck down by life circumstances, but through his steady faith in Christ, he was never destroyed.

When his body was pushed to the absolute limit in a rough environment, he learned to rely on God's grace to keep him on his feet.

To become a mentally tough athlete, you should look for ways to make your practice uncomfortable.

If you play basketball, stop only shooting in nice, air-conditioned gyms. Go outside and play street ball on an uneven court with a rusty double-rim hoop and a slick, worn-out basketball. If you play soccer, find a bumpy, muddy field to practice your footwork instead of a perfect turf complex. If you play baseball or softball, field ground balls on a rocky dirt patch where the ball takes wild, unpredictable hops.

Why is this so important?

Because perfect conditions are a luxury and one of the worst things that you can do when you are trying to improve your skills. When you only practice in cushy environments with flawless equipment, it tells your subconscious mind to power down, thinking you have already achieved greatness and no longer need to fight for it. However, training in tough environments is a signal to your mind to work harder; the goal is still out of reach.

Practicing rough also teaches you to stop relying on everything going exactly your way. It forces your brain to adapt to chaos, kills your excuses, and teaches you how to focus through uncertainty.

When you intentionally practice in tough, uncomfortable, and chaotic environments, you build a mental armor that makes playing in normal conditions feel completely effortless.

Limitation 3: Practicing Smaller - Lionel Messi

When you watch Lionel Messi play soccer, it looks like the game is moving in slow motion for him. While twenty-one other players are frantically running around a massive grass field, Messi calmly weaves through defenders with impossible, flawless precision.

How does he process the game so much faster than everyone else? He developed his elite skills by playing "smaller."

Before he was dominating in full-sized professional stadiums, Messi spent his childhood in Argentina playing a game called Futsal. Futsal is a version of soccer played on a tiny, hard court that is roughly the size of a basketball court.

But the court is not the only thing that is smaller. The game is played with a ball that is significantly smaller, heavier, and bounces much less than a standard soccer ball.

When you play in a space that small, your brain is literally forced to work overtime. You do not have fifty yards of open grass to sprint into. The moment you touch the ball on a tiny court, defenders are instantly in your face. To survive in that cramped environment, Messi had to develop incredibly fast reflexes, lightning-quick decision-making, and tiny, precise touches on the ball. Playing with smaller equipment in a tight space forces the nervous system to adapt to extreme pressure.

By the time Messi stepped onto a massive, full-sized professional soccer field, the game felt incredibly slow to him. Because his brain was already used to surviving in a tight box, a regular field felt like an ocean of endless time and space.

This shows the truth of 2 Corinthians 4:8-9, which says we are "hard pressed on every side, but not crushed; perplexed, but not in despair." When you play in a tiny space with smaller equipment, you are literally hard pressed by the defense and the boundaries. The speed of the game is frustrating and perplexing.

But Messi, whose deep Catholic faith keeps him incredibly grounded, did not let the tight pressure crush him. He points both index fingers to heaven after every single goal he scores, acknowledging that God gave him his abilities. He embraced being pressed on every side on those tiny Futsal courts, trusting that God uses our tightest, most uncomfortable physical and mental situations to build our greatest strengths.

If you want to speed up your brain, improve your physical reflexes, and build elite technical skills, you have to intentionally shrink your environment.

Play 3v3 basketball in a tiny, restricted corner of the driveway. Use a skinny, wooden training bat to hit bolt balls instead of real baseballs. Play soccer in a tight school hallway (get permission first).

When you deliberately practice in tighter spaces and use smaller equipment, your brain must work twice as hard to handle the lack of space. When game day finally arrives and you are back on a normal field with normal equipment, your brain will process the game flawlessly, and everything will feel like it is moving in slow motion, just like Messi.

Limitation 4: Slow Intentional Training - Katie Ledecky

While most people focus on speed and immediate results, the greatest athletes secretly focus on going slow.

Katie Ledecky is the most dominant female swimmer in Olympic history. She shatters world records and wins Olympic gold medals by swimming at a pace that breaks the will of her competitors.

The secret to her unstoppable speed on race day is her intense dedication to extremely slow, intentional training during practice.

Ledecky is famous for practicing a drill where she swims lengths of the pool with a plastic cup balanced perfectly on top of her head. If she rushes her stroke, drops her elbow, or moves her head even a fraction of an inch out of alignment, the cup falls off. To keep the cup perfectly balanced, she has to swim at a painfully slow, highly intentional pace. She breaks down every single micro movement of her stroke until it is locked deep into her brain and muscle memory.

Slowing down her training forces her to feel her exact mechanics in the water. It exposes her weaknesses and removes momentum, forcing her muscles to work perfectly. By mastering the slow, boring reps, she builds a flawless technique that leads to explosive speed during race time.

Ledecky's intense discipline is fueled by her strong faith and prayer life. Before every single race, she centers herself through prayer. This spiritual routine gives her the calm mindset required to handle extreme physical pain. In 2 Corinthians, we are reminded that we will be hard pressed on every side. Slow, intentional training is incredibly frustrating and presses hard against our natural desire to rush through practice. But faith in God gives her the patience to endure the slow, unglamorous work. She trusts that the tedious, slow reps are not a punishment, but a necessary process to refine the gifts God has given her.

Let's bring this to your life. Do not just rush through your drills so you can scrimmage. If you want to master a physical skill, you have to practice it at half speed. Shoot a basketball slowly to feel your wrist snap. Swing your golf club in slow motion to feel your hip rotation.

Slow reps expose your flaws and force you to fix them. Master the boring, slow details in your practice, and you will become explosive and unstoppable in the game.

The Proof Behind the Drill & Why It Matters

When you intentionally limit your resources and spaces, train in rough environments, or slow down your repetitions, you trigger a powerful biological and psychological response in your brain.

Psychologists call this the theory of "Desirable Difficulties," a concept pioneered by cognitive psychologist Dr. Robert Bjork at UCLA in 1994. His research shows that when you make a learning environment artificially harder or more restrictive, your brain is forced to work significantly harder to solve the problem. If you practice hitting a baseball with a heavy, wooden broomstick instead of a lightweight, expensive bat, your brain is forced to recruit more neural pathways to make contact. This intense struggle creates deeper, more permanent learning in your motor cortex.

When you return to using normal equipment, the task feels incredibly easy because your brain has already adapted to a much higher level of difficulty. This directly supports the first two pillars of Training With Less and Playing Rough.

In sports science, playing with limitations is also known as the Constraint-Led Approach. When you place a physical constraint on an athlete, like playing in a smaller, restrictive space like Lionel Messi in Futsal, you force their nervous system to invent new, creative ways to succeed. Messi playing in small, confined courts was a constraint that forced his brain to develop elite agility, quickness, clean footwork, and fast decision-making to survive.

Also, Katie Ledecky's slow intentional training is backed by the science of "myelination." As seen in Daniel Coyle's research on skill acquisition, every time you fire a neural circuit perfectly, your brain wraps that nerve fiber in a conductive substance called myelin. The thicker the myelin gets, the faster and more accurately your muscles react.

Myelin only grows when the technique is executed with absolute perfection.

So if you rush through practice with sloppy form, you build sloppy myelin. By forcing yourself to do slow, highly intentional reps, you guarantee perfect mechanics, which builds a thick layer of myelin and creates a flawless, automatic reflex on game day.

3-Minute Mindset Drill #7: Train with Less, Practice Tough and Tight, Master Slow Reps

Use this drill before your physical practice to intentionally design a limitation that will push your brain and body to learn faster and refine your skills.

Step 1: Pick Your Limitation. Decide which of the four limitations you will focus on today. Will you Train With Less, Practice Tough, Play Smaller, or use Slow Intentional Training? Pick only one for the day.

Step 2: Build the Constraint. Create a specific physical limitation for your practice today. If you chose "Train With Less," practice dribbling with a tennis ball. If you chose "Practice Tough," take ground balls fielding with your bare hands. If you choose "Slow Intentional Training," execute ten pitches or ten golf swings at exactly half speed with perfect mechanics. You get the idea.

Step 3: Set a Limitation Goal. Do not just casually practice with your new constraint; give yourself a specific, measurable target to hit while working under that restriction. For example, you might set a goal to complete ten perfect passes into a target that is exactly 2/3rds the normal size. If you are playing rough, your goal might be to cleanly field fifteen ground balls on a rocky dirt patch without a single error. Setting a hard number forces you to lock in your focus and fight through the frustration until the limitation goal is crushed.

Step 4: Execute the Reps. Step onto the field or court and complete your physical practice while working through the limitation. When you get frustrated, remind yourself that the extreme difficulty is actively rewiring your brain and muscle memory for top performance.

Step 5: Connect to Scripture. Read 2 Corinthians 4:8-9 out loud. Remind yourself that today's intentional limitation will press you hard, but it will not crush you. It is building your unbreakable mindset.

The Mindset Check

George Foreman chopped wood to become the oldest heavyweight champion. Manny Pacquiao fought barefoot in the dirt to build an unbreakable chin. Lionel Messi played on small courts to become unguardable. Katie Ledecky swims at painfully slow speeds to shatter world records. They all used limitations to become legends.

Reflection Questions:

What is one piece of fancy equipment you can completely eliminate from your practice this week to force yourself to work harder?

Are you rushing through your practice reps, or are you willing to slow down half speed and master the boring details?

Parents Coaching Corner

Parents, we naturally want to give our children the absolute best of everything. We want to buy them the three-hundred-dollar bats, the customized gear, and the expensive private lessons to give them an edge in their sport.

But the science of Desirable Difficulties shows us that sometimes, giving them too much actually stunts their athletic growth.

Do not be afraid to let your athlete train with less. Athletes do not need expensive equipment or a fancy batting cage to outwork their competition.

If they complain that their practice field is bumpy or their equipment is old, do not immediately rush to buy them a replacement. Use it as a coaching moment. Tell them that playing basketball with a rusty rim, running on a rough field or swimming at the local YMCA is exactly what builds mental toughness.

Encourage them to try the Limitation Code. By allowing them to struggle slightly and adapt to less than perfect conditions, you are helping them build a gritty, resilient mindset that no amount of money could ever buy.

Chapter Summary

Take On the Struggle: Training with less equipment or in rough environments strips away excuses and builds raw, authentic mental toughness.

Embrace the Tight Spaces: Do not always practice with endless room. Playing in a smaller, restricted area forces you to make lightning-fast decisions and master precise movements, so the game feels incredibly slow and easy when you return to a full-sized court.

Slow Down to Speed Up: Rushing through sloppy practice reps builds sloppy myelin and bad habits. Slow, highly intentional training exposes your flaws and helps build perfect technique.

The Science of Desirable Difficulties: Artificially making your training harder forces your brain to work overtime, which results in faster and more permanent physical improvement.

Mindset Drill #7: In your practices, intentionally design a limitation that will push your brain and body to learn faster and refine your skills.

Pressed But Not Crushed: As 2 Corinthians 4:8-9 teaches, the physical limitations and struggles you face are not meant to destroy you. With faith, those struggles are the exact tools God uses to build your unbreakable character and mindset.

Closing Prayer

Thank You, Lord, for the challenges and the limitations in my life. Help me to stop complaining about what I do not have and teach me how to maximize the unique gifts You have already given me. When I am hard pressed by tough competition or difficult environments, remind me that I am not crushed. Give me the discipline to slow down, embrace the hard work, and build my skills the right way. Amen.

Additional Mindset Tools & Resources

The Obstacle Is the Way: *The Timeless Art of Turning Trials into Triumph* by Ryan Holiday. This book is a great look at how some of the most successful people in history used big limitations, disadvantages, and tough times as the exact fuel they needed to achieve greatness.

BUILT FOR WHAT'S NEXT

You have officially made it to the end of this training manual, but your real journey is just beginning.

When you started this book, you already had the physical talent, the speed, and the drive to compete. But now, you have something that most young athletes will never take the time to develop. You have a mentally tough unbreakable mind.

Throughout these pages, you have been given the exact mental codes used by the greatest champions in the world. You learned that true greatness does not start on the scoreboard. It starts with the **Identity Code**, where you intentionally decide who you are and feed your subconscious mind with positive truth. You mastered the **Game Plan Code**, taking your big dreams out of your head and writing them down to build a roadmap through adversity. You discovered the **Blueprint Code**, which taught you to activate your mirror neurons by studying the elite athletes who came before you.

When performance anxiety tries to creep in, you now have the ultimate defense. You know how to use the **Visualization Code** to vividly rehearse your performance before you ever step onto the field. When the pressure gets incredibly heavy, you will use the **Composure Code** to take a tactical, deep breath sequence. This resets your nervous system and invites God's peace into the moment.

Instead of letting the noise of the crowd or the fear of a mistake paralyze you, you will use the **Quiet Mind Code** to silence the chaos and get into the zone. Finally, you learned how to use the **Limitations Code**. This proves that training with less and smaller, practicing rough, and slowing down your mechanics are the tools to speed up learning and improve your skills.

So, what is the ultimate benefit of all this mental training?

The benefit is freedom. When you apply these seven faith-fueled mindset drills to your daily routine, you will no longer play with a tight, fearful, or anxious mindset. You will no longer let one mistake ruin your game or entire week. You will bounce back faster, compete with steady confidence, and perform under pressure like it is just another normal day at practice.

This mental armor toolkit was built to protect your love of the sport, improve your physical performance, and constantly remind you that your worth is anchored in Christ, not in your statistics.

You have put in the hard work. You have trained your body, and you have trained your mind.

You are focused. You are mentally tough. You are prepared. **You are unbreakable.**

OUR SINCERE GRATITUDE

Thank you for being a part of this mission to raise the next generation of faith-driven champions!

If this mental toughness guide has helped you or your young athlete grow in faith, rise above challenges, and play better under pressure, we'd love to hear your thoughts to help inspire the next young athlete.

Your feedback doesn't just help us spread the good news—it helps other athletes find the encouragement, mental strength, and biblical truth they need to thrive in both sports and life.

Please scan the QR' code below with your phone to go to the review page for this book. Thank you, we greatly appreciate it!

SCRIPTURE SOURCES

Throughout this book, Scripture passages are presented from a variety of Bible translations to enhance understanding and strengthen each message. The translations included are the New International Version (NIV), English Standard Version (ESV), and New Living Translation (NLT). These verses were thoughtfully selected to clearly convey biblical truth in a way that connects with athletes who are struggling with their injury and current recovery timeline. Used by permission. All rights reserved.

Biblica, Inc. (2011). *The Holy Bible: New International Version.* (Original work published 1973). Biblica, Inc.

Crossway. (2001). *The Holy Bible: English Standard Version.* Crossway Bibles.

Tyndale House Foundation. (2015). *The Holy Bible: New Living Translation.* (Original work published 1996). Tyndale House Publishers, Inc.

www.ingramcontent.com/pod-product-compliance
Lightning Source LLC
Chambersburg PA
CBHW061044050726
47592CB00004B/1583